EXPERIENCE NETHERLANDS TRAVEL PREPARATION GUIDE

DELZY HAMPTON

TABLE OF CONTENT

CHAPTER ONE

THE NETHERLANDS EXPERIENCE

The Netherlands, also known as Holland, is a country located in northwestern Europe. It is famous for its flat landscape, tulip fields, windmills, cheese, and world-renowned art museums. The country has a rich cultural heritage and a vibrant modern society, making it a popular destination for tourists and expatriates.

The Netherlands is one of the most densely populated countries in Europe, with a population of over 17 million people. The majority of the population is concentrated in the western part of the country, which is home to the major cities of Amsterdam, Rotterdam, and The Hague. These cities are the centres of finance, commerce, and politics in the Netherlands, and they offer a unique blend of modern and historic architecture, as well as a thriving cultural scene.

One of the most striking features of the Netherlands is its flat landscape. The country is situated on the delta of several rivers, including the Rhine and the Meuse, and much of it lies below sea level. This unique geography has led to the development of a sophisticated system of dikes, dams, and canals that protect the land from flooding. The country is also known for its beautiful countryside, which is dotted with charming villages, rolling fields, and picturesque windmills.

The Dutch are famous for their love of bicycles, and it is not uncommon to see cyclists everywhere, from the bustling cities to the rural countryside. The country has an extensive network of bike lanes and is considered one of the most bicycle-friendly countries in the world. In addition, the Netherlands is home to one of the world's most extensive and efficient public transportation systems, making it easy to get around.

The Netherlands is renowned for its contributions to the arts, particularly during the Dutch Golden Age in the 17th century. During this time, the country produced some of the world's most famous artists, including Rembrandt, Vermeer, and Hals.

Today, the country continues to celebrate its rich cultural heritage, and many of its museums and galleries are world-famous, including the Rijksmuseum in Amsterdam, the Mauritshuis in The Hague, and the Van Gogh Museum.

One of the most notable aspects of Dutch society is its tolerant and progressive attitudes. The Netherlands was the first country in the world to legalize same-sex marriage, and it is widely recognized as one of the most accepting and liberal countries in the world. This progressive spirit is reflected in the country's vibrant nightlife and diverse cultural scene, as well as its commitment to sustainability and environmental protection.

Despite its many charms, the Netherlands is not without its challenges. Like many other developed countries, it faces issues such as income inequality, housing shortages, and a growing ageing population. However, the country is well known for its innovative and forward-thinking approach to these challenges, and it is widely considered to be a leader in fields such as renewable energy, water management, and healthcare.

In conclusion, the Netherlands is a unique and fascinating country that offers a rich cultural heritage, a vibrant modern society, and a stunning natural landscape. Whether you're interested in art, history, nature, or just looking for a fun and relaxed way of life, the Netherlands has something to offer everyone.

WHAT TO EAT AND DRINK IN NETHERLAND

The cuisine of the Netherlands is often described as hearty and simple, reflecting the country's historical roots as a seafaring and farming nation. The traditional Dutch diet consists of potatoes, vegetables, and meat, with fish and cheese playing an important role. In recent years, however, the country's dining scene has become much more diverse, reflecting its cosmopolitan nature and the influence of international cuisine.

One of the most iconic foods in the Netherlands is the "stamppot," a hearty dish made from mashed potatoes mixed with various ingredients, such as carrots, onions, or kale. Another staple is the "erwtensoep," a thick pea soup that is traditionally served with slices of smoked sausage. These dishes are typically served with a slice of bread and are often enjoyed in the winter months.

Cheese is another important part of Dutch cuisine, and the country is famous for its Gouda and Edam cheeses, which are produced using traditional methods and are available in a range of ages and flavours. The Dutch are also known for their love of stroopwafels, a sweet treat made from thin wafers filled with syrup.

When it comes to drinks, the Netherlands is famous for its beer. The country has a long brewing tradition, and its beers are known for their high quality and wide range of flavours. Some of the most popular brands include Heineken, Grolsch, and Amstel. The Dutch also produce a wide range of spirits, including jenever, a gin-like spirit that is traditionally served straight or mixed with lemon and sugar.

In recent years, the Dutch dining scene has become much more diverse, reflecting the country's cosmopolitan nature and the influence of international cuisine. In Amsterdam, for example, you can find everything from traditional Dutch restaurants to Thai, Italian, and Chinese eateries. The city is also home to a thriving street food scene, with a variety of food trucks offering everything from Dutch pancakes to falafel.

In addition to its traditional cuisine, the Netherlands is also known for its coffee culture. The country has a long history of coffee-drinking, and coffee shops can be found in almost every city and town. Dutch coffee is typically strong and flavorful, and is often served with a piece of cake or a biscuit.

When it comes to dining out, the Netherlands has a wide range of options, from casual cafes and fast food joints to fine dining restaurants. In the cities, you can find everything from street food and food trucks to high-end restaurants, and there is something to suit every budget and taste.

The Netherlands has a rich culinary tradition that is reflected in its hearty, simple cuisine, as well as its love of cheese, beer, and coffee. Whether you're looking for traditional Dutch dishes or international cuisine, the country has something to offer every food lover. With its thriving street food scene, cosmopolitan cities, and high-end restaurants, the Netherlands is a foodie's paradise, and is sure to satisfy even the most discerning palate.

WHAT TO BUY IN NETHERLANDS

The Netherlands is a shopper's paradise, offering a wide range of products to suit every taste and budget. Whether you're looking for traditional Dutch souvenirs or high-end designer goods, you're sure to find something that appeals to you. Here are some of the best things to buy in the Netherlands.

1. Dutch cheeses: The Netherlands is famous for its cheese, and there are a wide range of delicious cheeses available to buy, including Gouda, Edam, and Leiden. Look for cheese shops and markets that offer a range of aged cheeses, as well as different flavours and varieties.

2. Delftware: Delftware is a type of blue-and-white pottery that originated in the Dutch city of Delft. You can find a wide range of Delftware products,

including plates, vases, and figurines, and it makes for a great souvenir.

3. Tulip bulbs: The Netherlands is famous for its tulips, and tulip bulbs are a popular item to buy. You can find tulip bulbs for sale in markets, flower shops, and online. Whether you're looking for traditional tulip bulbs or more unusual varieties, you're sure to find something that appeals to you.

4. Dutch clogs: Wooden clogs are an iconic symbol of the Netherlands, and make for a great souvenir. You can find a wide range of clogs, including traditional wooden clogs and more

modern designs, in markets and souvenir shops.

5. Stroopwafels: Stroopwafels are a type of waffle that originated in the Netherlands. They are made from thin wafers filled with syrup, and make for a delicious snack. Look for stroopwafels in markets, bakeries, and supermarkets.

6. Dutch gin: Jenever is a gin-like spirit that is popular in the Netherlands. It is typically served straight or mixed with lemon and sugar, and is a must-try for gin lovers. You can find jenever in liquor stores and bars.

7. Dutch designer goods: The Netherlands is home to a thriving fashion scene, and you can find a wide range of high-end designer goods, including clothing, accessories, and home decor. Look for boutiques and department stores in cities like Amsterdam and Rotterdam for the best shopping options.

8. Dutch art: The Netherlands has a rich art tradition, and you can find a wide range of artworks for sale, including paintings, sculptures, and prints. Look for art galleries and museums in cities like Amsterdam and The Hague for the best selection.

9. Dutch bikes: Bikes are a popular mode of transportation in the Netherlands, and you can find a wide range of bikes for sale, including city bikes, racing bikes, and electric bikes. Look for bike shops in cities like Amsterdam and Utrecht for the best selection.

10. Dutch souvenirs: There is a wide range of Dutch souvenirs available, including keychains, postcards, magnets, and T-shirts. Look for souvenir shops and markets in cities like Amsterdam and Rotterdam for the best selection.

The Netherlands is a great place to buy souvenirs and gifts, as well as high-end designer goods and traditional Dutch products. Whether you're looking for cheese, pottery, or tulip bulbs, you're sure to find something that appeals to you in this vibrant and cosmopolitan country.

BEST MUSEUMS IN NETHERLAND

The Netherlands is home to many museums that showcase its history, art, and science. Here are some of the best museums in the Netherlands that are worth visiting:

1. Rijksmuseum, Amsterdam: This is the largest and most famous museum in the Netherlands, which was

established in 1885. It is home to over 8,000 objects of Dutch art and history, including works by Rembrandt, Vermeer, and Frans Hals.

2. Van Gogh Museum, Amsterdam: This museum is dedicated to the life and works of Vincent van Gogh, one of the most famous Dutch painters. It has the largest collection of van Gogh's paintings in the world and attracts over 2 million visitors annually.

3. Stedelijk Museum, Amsterdam: This is the largest museum of modern and contemporary art in the Netherlands, which was established in 1895. It has a vast collection of works by artists such

as Pablo Picasso, Joan Miró, and Willem de Kooning.

4. Mauritshuis, The Hague: This is a small but world-renowned museum that is housed in a beautiful 17th-century palace. It has a collection of Dutch and Flemish paintings from the Golden Age, including works by Vermeer, Rembrandt, and Frans Hals.

5. Museum Boijmans Van Beuningen, Rotterdam: This museum is one of the oldest and largest in the Netherlands, which was founded in 1849. It has an extensive collection of Dutch and European art from the Middle Ages to

the present day, including works by Rembrandt, Bosch, and Rubens.

6. Kröller-Müller Museum, Otterlo: This museum is located in the beautiful Hoge Veluwe National Park and is dedicated to the works of Vincent van Gogh. It has the second-largest collection of van Gogh's paintings in the world, as well as works by other artists such as Pablo Picasso, Georges Seurat, and Piet Mondrian.

7. Museum Catharijneconvent, Utrecht: This is the largest museum of Christian art in the Netherlands, which was established in 1883. It has a vast collection of religious artifacts,

including illuminated manuscripts, sculptures, and gold and silver objects.

8. Dutch National Maritime Museum, Amsterdam: This museum is dedicated to the maritime history of the Netherlands, including its ships, navigation, and trade. It has a vast collection of objects, including model ships, paintings, and navigation instruments.

9. Naturalis Biodiversity Center, Leiden: This museum is dedicated to the natural history of the world, with a focus on the Netherlands. It has a collection of over 37 million

specimens, including fossils, insects, and plants.

10. Nationaal Oorlogs- en Verzetsmuseum, Amsterdam: This museum is dedicated to the history of war and resistance in the Netherlands, from the Middle Ages to the present day. It has a vast collection of objects, including weapons, photographs, and personal stories.

These museums are just a few of the many excellent museums in the Netherlands that are worth visiting. Whether you are interested in art, history, science, or culture, you will find something to suit your interests in this beautiful country.

BEST CHURCHES IN NETHERLANDS

There are many historic and architecturally beautiful churches located throughout the country. Here is a list of some of the best churches in the Netherlands:

1. Oude Kerk (Old Church) in Amsterdam: This church is the oldest building in Amsterdam and is considered one of the most beautiful examples of Gothic architecture in the Netherlands. It dates back to the 13th century and is a popular tourist

attraction, with a rich history and beautiful stained glass windows.

2. Grote Kerk (Great Church) in Haarlem: This is the largest church in Haarlem and one of the oldest in the Netherlands. It was built in the 14th century and has a beautiful Gothic interior, complete with a magnificent organ and numerous works of art.

3. Sint-Janskerk (St. John's Church) in Gouda: This is a beautiful Gothic church located in the centre of Gouda. It is known for its impressive stained glass windows and its elaborate wooden pulpit, which is considered

one of the finest examples of Renaissance art in the Netherlands.

4. Dom Tower in Utrecht: This is the tallest church tower in the Netherlands and is a popular tourist attraction in Utrecht. It dates back to the 14th century and offers stunning views of the city from the top.

5. Sint-Bavokerk (St. Bavo's Church) in Haarlem: This is a beautiful Gothic church that dates back to the 13th century. It is known for its impressive organ and its beautiful stained glass windows, as well as its rich history.

6. Sint-Jacobskerk (St. James's Church) in The Hague: This is a beautiful

Gothic church located in the centre of The Hague. It is known for its stunning stained glass windows and its rich history, which includes being used as a place of worship for over 700 years.

7. Sint-Servaasbasiliek (St. Servatius Basilica) in Maastricht: This is a beautiful basilica that dates back to the 9th century and is one of the oldest churches in the Netherlands. It is known for its beautiful stained glass windows, elaborate frescoes, and its rich history.

8. Onze-Lieve-Vrouwebasiliek (Basilica of Our Lady) in Antwerp: This is a

beautiful basilica located in Antwerp, Belgium, which is just a short distance from the Netherlands. It is known for its stunning Gothic architecture, rich history, and it's beautiful stained glass windows.

These are just a few of the many beautiful and historic churches located throughout the Netherlands. Each of these churches offers a unique glimpse into the country's rich religious heritage and serves as a testament to the beauty and history of this fascinating country. Whether you are a religious person or simply appreciate beautiful architecture, there is something to be enjoyed by everyone at these magnificent churches.

BEST MOSQUES IN NETHERLANDS

The Netherlands is home to a diverse community of Muslims, and there are several mosques that serve the religious needs of the community. Here are some of the best mosques in the Netherlands:

1. Al-Fourqaan Mosque: Al-Fourqaan Mosque is located in Rotterdam and is considered one of the largest and most beautiful mosques in the Netherlands. The mosque is designed in a traditional Islamic architectural style

and features a spacious prayer hall, a large dome, and several minarets.

2. As-Soennah Mosque: As-Soennah Mosque is located in The Hague and is one of the largest and most influential mosques in the Netherlands. The mosque offers a range of religious and cultural activities, including religious education for children, youth programs, and community events.

3. Al-Tawheed Mosque: Al-Tawheed Mosque is located in Amsterdam and is one of the most well-known and respected mosques in the Netherlands. The mosque is well-known for its welcoming

atmosphere, its community outreach programs, and its strong commitment to promoting Islamic values and traditions.

4. Al-Hidayah Mosque: Al-Hidayah Mosque is located in Utrecht and is known for its beautiful architecture and its active community programs. The mosque offers a range of services, including religious education, community events, and social support services for families and individuals in need.

5. Al-Fath Mosque: Al-Fath Mosque is located in Rotterdam and is one of the largest and most active mosques in the

Netherlands. The mosque is well-known for its warm and welcoming atmosphere, its strong commitment to community service, and its emphasis on promoting Islamic values and traditions.

6. Al-Jaami Mosque: Al-Jaami Mosque is located in Amsterdam and is one of the oldest and most respected mosques in the Netherlands. The mosque is well-known for its traditional Islamic architecture, its rich history, and its commitment to promoting Islamic values and traditions.

7. Al-Furqan Mosque: Al-Furqan Mosque is located in The Hague and is one of the largest and most active mosques in the Netherlands. The mosque offers a range of religious and cultural activities, including religious education, community events, and social support services for families and individuals in need.

These are some of the best mosques in the Netherlands. Each mosque is unique in its own way and offers a range of services and programs that are designed to meet the needs of the local community. Whether you are looking for a place to pray, learn about

Islam, or connect with other Muslims, you are sure to find what you are looking for at one of these great mosques.

BEST PARKS AND GARDENS IN NETHERLAND

The Netherlands is known for its scenic beauty, parks, and gardens. There are many parks and gardens in the Netherlands, each offering a unique experience. Some of the best parks and gardens in Netherlands are:

1. Keukenhof Gardens: Located in Lisse, this park is a famous tourist attraction, particularly for its tulips. Every spring, the park is filled with a colourful array of tulips, daffodils,

hyacinths, and other flowers. The park is spread over an area of 32 hectares and has a large lake, windmills, and beautiful sculptures.

2. Het Loo Palace Garden: This is a beautiful baroque garden located in Apeldoorn. The garden is spread over an area of 100 hectares and has beautiful flower beds, lawns, and trees. There are also several lakes and fountains in the garden.

3. Vondelpark: This is a large public park located in Amsterdam and is one of the most popular parks in the city. The park has a large lake, a theatre, several playgrounds, and several restaurants.

The park is surrounded by beautiful trees and is a popular place for picnics and outdoor activities.

4. Trompenburg Tuinen en Arboretum: This garden is located in Rotterdam and is famous for its collection of exotic plants and trees. The garden has a large collection of rhododendrons, azaleas, and other shrubs. There are also several greenhouses in the garden where you can see tropical plants and flowers.

5. Hoge Veluwe National Park: This is a large nature reserve located in Gelderland and is one of the largest national parks in the Netherlands. The

park is spread over an area of 5,500 hectares and has a large collection of wildlife, including deer, boars, and foxes. There are also several hiking trails in the park and a museum dedicated to the work of the Dutch painter Vincent van Gogh.

6. Wilhelmina Park: This is a large park located in Utrecht and is one of the oldest parks in the Netherlands. The park has a large lake, several flower beds, and a beautiful rose garden. There are also several playgrounds and a petting zoo in the park.

7. Aalsmeer Flower Auction Garden: This garden is located in Aalsmeer and

is famous for its flower auctions. The garden has a large collection of flowers, including tulips, roses, and lilies. There is also a museum in the garden that showcases the history of flower trading in the Netherlands.

8. Burgers' Zoo: This is a large zoo located in Arnhem and is one of the largest zoos in the Netherlands. The zoo has a large collection of animals, including lions, elephants, and giraffes. There are also several aquariums in the zoo, where you can see a variety of fish and marine life.

9. Arboretum Trompenburg: This is a beautiful arboretum located in

Rotterdam and is famous for its collection of trees and shrubs. The arboretum has a large collection of conifers, deciduous trees, and shrubs, including rhododendrons, azaleas, and magnolias. There are also several greenhouses in the arboretum where you can see tropical plants and flowers.

10. Oostvaardersplassen: This is a large nature reserve located in Flevoland and is one of the largest nature reserves in the Netherlands. The reserve has a large collection of wildlife, including deer, boars, and birds. There are several hiking trails in

the reserve, as well as a visitor centre where you can learn more about the wildlife and the history of the area.

The Netherlands has a wealth of parks and gardens, each offering a unique experience. Whether you're interested in flowers, wildlife, or just enjoying a peaceful day in nature, there's a park or garden in the Netherlands that's perfect for you. These parks and gardens are a testament to the country's commitment to preserving and enhancing its natural beauty, and are a must-visit for anyone who loves nature and the great outdoors.

BEST ART GALLERIES IN NETHERLAND

The Netherlands is a hub for contemporary art and boasts some of the best art galleries in the world. take a look at some of the top art galleries in the country:

1. Stedelijk Museum Amsterdam: This museum is the largest museum for modern and contemporary art in the Netherlands, and is known for its impressive collection of modern art. Some of the artists featured here include Pablo Picasso, Vincent van Gogh, and Kazimir Malevich.

2. Rijksmuseum: This museum is the largest museum in the Netherlands and is home to an impressive collection of Dutch masterpieces. It is most famous for its collection of works by Rembrandt, Vermeer, and Frans Hals, as well as its collection of decorative arts.

3. Van Gogh Museum: This museum is dedicated to the life and works of Vincent van Gogh, and features the largest collection of his works in the world. Visitors can see masterpieces such as "The Starry Night" and "Sunflowers".

4. Boijmans Van Beuningen Museum: This museum is one of the oldest and largest museums in the Netherlands and is known for its impressive collection of old master paintings, modern and contemporary art, and design.

5. Museum De Lakenhal: This museum is one of the oldest art museums in the Netherlands and is known for its collection of Dutch Golden Age paintings, including works by Rembrandt, Vermeer, and Frans Hals.

6. Kröller-Müller Museum: This museum is located in the Hoge Veluwe National Park and is known for its collection of

19th- and 20th-century art. It is home to one of the largest collections of Vincent van Gogh's works outside of the Van Gogh Museum in Amsterdam.

7. Museum Catharijneconvent: This museum is the national museum of Christian art and cultural history in the Netherlands and features an impressive collection of mediaeval and Renaissance art.

8. Foam Fotografiemuseum Amsterdam: This museum is dedicated to contemporary photography and features an impressive collection of works by both established and emerging photographers.

9. Nederlands Fotomuseum: This museum is dedicated to the history of photography in the Netherlands and features an impressive collection of works by Dutch photographers.

10. M - Museum Leuven: This museum is the largest art museum in Belgium and is known for its collection of Belgian art from the Middle Ages to the present day.

The Netherlands is a hub for contemporary art and boasts some of the best art galleries in the world. From the Stedelijk Museum Amsterdam to the Nederlands Fotomuseum, there's something for everyone to enjoy.

Whether you're a fan of old master paintings, modern art, or contemporary photography, you'll find an impressive collection at one of these top art galleries in the Netherlands.

CHAPTER TWO

TRAVEL SMART

THINGS TO KNOW BEFORE VISITING NETHERLANDS

Here are some important things to know before visiting the Netherlands.

1. Geography: The Netherlands is a small, flat country located in the coastal plain of northwest Europe. The country is bounded by the North Sea to the north and west, Germany to the east, and Belgium to the south.

2. Climate: The Netherlands has a maritime climate, characterised by mild winters and cool summers. The average temperature in the summer is around 20°C (68°F) and in the winter it is around 5°C (41°F). It can also be

quite rainy and windy, especially in the coastal areas.

3. Population: The population of the Netherlands is around 17.3 million people. The country is known for its diverse and multicultural population, with many different ethnicities, nationalities, and languages represented.

4. Language: The official language of the Netherlands is Dutch, although many people also speak English, especially in tourist areas.

5. Currency: The currency used in the Netherlands is the Euro (EUR).

6. Transportation: The Netherlands has an excellent transportation system, with well-developed roads, trains, and public transportation. The country is also known for its extensive network of bike paths and many people choose to travel by bike, especially in urban areas.

7. Food and Drink: The Dutch cuisine is hearty and traditional, with many dishes centred around potatoes, cheese, and meat. Some popular dishes include stamppot (mashed potatoes with vegetables), hutspot (a type of stew), and stroopwafels (syrup waffles). The country is also known for its beer, with many local microbreweries producing a variety of styles.

8. Culture and History: The Netherlands has a rich cultural and historical heritage, with many museums, galleries, and historic sites to explore. Some of the most famous museums in the country include the Van Gogh Museum in Amsterdam and the Mauritshuis in The Hague.

9. Nightlife: The Netherlands has a vibrant nightlife, with many bars, clubs, and music venues to explore. Amsterdam, in particular, is known

for its lively nightlife scene and is a popular destination for party-goers.

10. Safety: The Netherlands is generally considered to be a safe country, with low levels of crime and a high standard of living. However, it is always important to take precautions and be aware of your surroundings, especially in busy tourist areas.

11. Tolerance and Diversity: The Netherlands is known for its liberal and progressive attitudes, and is a very tolerant and diverse country. Amsterdam, in particular, is known for its vibrant gay and lesbian community, and for its liberal attitudes towards sex and drugs.

12. Sustainability: The Netherlands is a leader in sustainable development, with many initiatives and policies aimed at reducing waste, conserving energy, and promoting sustainable transportation.

The Netherlands is a small country with a rich cultural heritage and many fascinating attractions to explore. Whether you're interested in history, art, food, or nightlife, the Netherlands has something to offer everyone. With its excellent transportation system, diverse population, and liberal attitudes, it is a great destination for travellers from all over the world.

GETTING HERE AND AROUND NETHERLANDS

The Netherlands is known for its well-developed transportation infrastructure, which includes various modes of transportation such as roadways, waterways, railways, and airways. The Dutch transportation system is efficient, convenient, and sustainable, and it plays a significant role in the country's economy and daily life.

Roadways:

The road network in the Netherlands is extensive and well-maintained, making it easy for residents and visitors to travel by car. The country has an extensive network of motorways, expressways, and local roads, with the majority of roads in good condition. The country also has a high number of roundabouts, which help to reduce traffic congestion and improve traffic flow.

Cycling:

Cycling is a popular mode of transportation in the Netherlands, and it is estimated that over a third of the Dutch population cycles to work or school on a daily basis. The country has an extensive network of dedicated cycle lanes and paths, making it safe and convenient to cycle around the country. The Dutch government has invested in infrastructure and facilities to encourage cycling, such as bike parking facilities and cycle repair shops.

Public Transport:

The public transport system in the Netherlands is highly developed and efficient, with a comprehensive network of trains, buses, and trams. The Dutch railways, operated by NS, are widely used by both residents and visitors, and the trains are fast, frequent, and reliable. The country's public transport system also includes a network of regional and intercity buses, which provide coverage to areas not served by trains. The trams in the cities, such as Amsterdam and Rotterdam, are a popular mode of transportation and serve as an alternative to the bus and train services.

Waterways:

The Netherlands is famous for its waterways, and the country has a well-developed network of canals, rivers, and lakes. In the past, waterways were the primary mode of transportation in the country, but today they are mainly used for recreational purposes. However, there are still some commercial vessels that use the waterways for transporting goods, such as containers and bulk cargo.

Airways:

The Netherlands has two main airports, Amsterdam Schiphol Airport and Rotterdam The Hague Airport, which serve as major hubs for both domestic and international travel. Schiphol is one of the busiest airports in Europe and handles millions of passengers each year. The airport is well-connected to the city centre and other parts of the country by train and bus services, making it easy to reach other destinations in the Netherlands.

The Netherlands has a well-developed transportation system that includes various modes of transportation, such as roadways, waterways, railways, and airways. The country's infrastructure is efficient, convenient, and sustainable, and it plays a significant role in the country's economy and daily life. The Dutch government has invested in infrastructure and facilities to encourage sustainable modes of transportation, such as cycling, and the country's public transport system is highly developed and efficient, making it easy for residents and visitors to travel around the country.

ESSENTIALS

Packing for a trip to the Netherlands can be a bit of a challenge, especially if it's your first time visiting the country. There are so many things to consider, including the weather, local customs, and the activities you have planned. To make the packing process a little easier, here is a comprehensive list of essentials to pack for your trip to the Netherlands.

   1. Clothing:

When it comes to clothing, it's essential to pack for the weather and the type of activities you have planned. The Netherlands has a moderate climate, with temperatures ranging from about 40°F to 70°F, so it's best to pack layers. Here are some clothing items you should consider:

- Light jackets: Pack a light rain jacket, windbreaker, or fleece for when the weather is cool or damp.
- Sweaters: Pack a few warm sweaters for when it gets chilly.
- Long-sleeved shirts: Pack a few long-sleeved shirts to wear during the day or when it's a bit cool.

- Jeans or trousers: Pack a few pairs of jeans or trousers that are comfortable and versatile.
- Shoes: Pack comfortable shoes for walking, as well as a pair of waterproof shoes for when it rains.
- Umbrella: Pack a compact and lightweight umbrella to keep you dry during those unexpected rain showers.
- Socks and underwear: Don't forget to pack enough socks and underwear for your trip.
- Scarf, hat, and gloves: Pack a warm scarf, hat, and gloves for when the weather is particularly chilly.
2. Toiletries:

When it comes to toiletries, it's best to pack the essentials, as well as any personal items you may need. Here are some items to consider:

- Toothbrush and toothpaste: Pack a toothbrush and toothpaste to keep your teeth clean and healthy.
- Shampoo and conditioner: Pack your favourite shampoo and conditioner to keep your hair clean and healthy.
- Soap and body wash: Pack your favourite soap and body wash to keep your skin clean and moisturised.
- Deodorant: Pack a deodorant to keep you feeling fresh and confident.

- Razor: If you need to shave, pack a razor and any necessary shaving cream.
- Makeup: Pack your favourite makeup items, such as foundation, mascara, and lipstick.
- Hairbrush or comb: Pack a hairbrush or comb to keep your hair looking neat and tidy.
- Sunscreen: Pack a high SPF sunscreen to protect your skin from the sun.
- Lip balm: Pack a lip balm to protect your lips from the elements.

3. Electronics:

The Netherlands is a modern country with excellent infrastructure, so you can expect to find most of the electronics you need. However, it's always a good idea to pack the essentials. Here are some items to consider:

- Phone and charger: Pack your phone and a charger to stay connected with friends and family back home.
- Laptop and charger: Pack your laptop and charger if you need to work or stay entertained while on the road.
- Camera: Pack a camera to capture all of the amazing memories you'll make in the Netherlands.

- Power adapter: Pack a power adapter that is compatible with the electrical outlets in the Netherlands.
- Headphones: Pack headphones to listen to music or watch movies without disturbing others.
4. Travel documents:

It's important to pack all of your travel documents and keep them in a safe and easily accessible place. Here are some items to consider:

- Passport: Pack your passport to enter the Netherlands and travel throughout Europe.

- Flight tickets: Pack your flight tickets to ensure you have all of the necessary information for your flights.
- Travel insurance: Pack your travel insurance documents to protect yourself in case of an emergency.
- Cash and credit cards: Pack cash and credit cards to pay for expenses during your trip.
5. Miscellaneous items:

There are a few other items that you may need during your trip to the Netherlands. Here are some items to consider:

- Map and guidebook: Pack a map and guidebook to help you navigate the country and learn about the local culture.

- Water bottle: Pack a reusable water bottle to stay hydrated while you explore.

- Travel pillow: Pack a travel pillow to ensure you get a comfortable night's sleep on the plane or train.

- Snacks: Pack some snacks to eat on the go or when you need a quick bite.

- First-aid kit: Pack a basic first-aid kit to treat any minor injuries or illnesses during your trip.

- Travel lock: Pack a travel lock to secure your luggage and keep your valuables safe.

packing for a trip to the Netherlands requires careful consideration of the weather, local customs, and your planned activities. By packing the essentials, such as clothing, toiletries, electronics, travel documents, and miscellaneous items, you'll be prepared for a fantastic and memorable trip.

GREAT ITINERARIES FOR NETHERLANDS

From charming canals, vibrant cities, and quaint countryside villages to rolling dunes, historic windmills, and iconic tulip fields, the Netherlands offers a range of experiences for travellers. Here are some itineraries to help you make the most of your visit to the Netherlands:

Amsterdam and its Surroundings:

1. Start your journey in Amsterdam, the country's lively capital city. Stroll along the historic canals, visit the Anne Frank House, and explore the many museums, including the Van Gogh Museum and the Rijksmuseum. Take a bike tour to see the city from a local's perspective and visit the Red

Light District to see a different side of Amsterdam.

Just outside of Amsterdam, you'll find the traditional Dutch village of Zaandijk, home to the famous Zaanse Schans windmills. The village also has several museums, including the Choco Museum, where you can learn about chocolate making, and the Clog Museum, where you can learn about the history of Dutch clogs.

In the evening, enjoy a dinner of traditional Dutch cuisine, such as stamppot (mashed potatoes with vegetables) or herring, and relax in one of Amsterdam's many coffee shops or bars.

The Dutch Coastline:

2. The Netherlands is famous for its long and beautiful coastline, dotted with charming seaside towns, sandy beaches, and dunes. Start your trip in The Hague, the seat of the Dutch government and home to the International Court of Justice. Explore the Binnenhof, the seat of the Dutch parliament, and visit the Mauritshuis Museum, which houses masterpieces by Vermeer, Rembrandt, and other Dutch Masters.

Next, head to Scheveningen, a popular seaside resort, for a walk along the pier, a visit to the SEA LIFE aquarium, or a dip in the North Sea. Continue to the charming fishing village of Katwijk and visit the Museum de Zwarte Tulp, which showcases the history of the tulip industry in the Netherlands.

Finally, end your trip in the trendy town of Zandvoort, famous for its wide sandy beach and bustling beach promenade.

The Dutch Countryside:

3. The Dutch countryside is dotted with picturesque villages, historic

windmills, and sprawling tulip fields. Start your trip in the charming village of Giethoorn, known as the "Venice of the Netherlands" for its network of canals and wooden bridges. Rent a boat and explore the village from the water or take a walk along the picturesque canal-side paths.

Next, visit the historic town of Zaanse Schans, home to a collection of well-preserved windmills and traditional Dutch houses. Take a tour of one of the windmills or visit the nearby cheese and clog factories to see how these traditional Dutch products are made.

Finally, head to the Keukenhof Gardens, one of the world's largest flower gardens, to see the fields of colourful tulips in bloom. The gardens are open from late April to mid-May and offer a breathtaking display of tulips, daffodils, and other spring flowers.

Whether you prefer the bustling city life of Amsterdam, the scenic coastline, or the tranquil countryside, the Netherlands offers a diverse range of experiences for visitors. Plan your itinerary and experience the best of what this charming country has to offer.

The Dutch Food Scene:

4. The Netherlands is home to a thriving food culture, with a variety of

traditional dishes and international cuisine. Start your culinary journey in Amsterdam, where you can sample Dutch cheeses, herring, and other traditional dishes. Be sure to visit the Albert Cuyp market, the largest outdoor market in the city, to sample local produce, cheeses, and street food.

Next, head to Rotterdam, the second-largest city in the Netherlands, where you'll find a thriving food scene with a focus on international cuisine. Visit the Markthal, a covered food market, to sample dishes from around the world, including Italian pizza, Moroccan tagine, and Indonesian satay.

Finally, end your trip in the picturesque village of Delft, famous for its traditional Dutch blue and white pottery. Take a cooking class to learn how to make traditional Dutch dishes, such as pea soup or stamppot, or visit one of the local restaurants to sample modern Dutch cuisine.

Dutch Festivals and Celebrations:

5. The Netherlands is home to a variety of festivals and celebrations throughout the year. Start your trip in

Amsterdam during the tulip season in April and May, when the city's many parks and public spaces are filled with colourful tulips. Take a tour of the tulip fields in the countryside or visit the Keukenhof Gardens to see the tulips in full bloom.

In August, head to the seaside town of Scheveningen for the annual kite-flying festival, where you'll see hundreds of colourful kites in the sky.

In December, visit the capital city of The Hague to experience the city's Christmas market, where you can sample traditional Dutch foods, such as oliebollen (doughnuts), and browse the festive stalls for gifts and souvenirs.

Whether you're interested in food, flowers, or festivities, the Netherlands has something for everyone. Plan your itinerary to coincide with one of these events for a truly unforgettable experience.

The Netherlands offers a diverse range of experiences for visitors, from bustling cities and charming countryside villages to scenic coastline and thriving food and culture scenes. Whether you prefer traditional Dutch culture or modern international cuisine, the Netherlands has something to offer everyone. Plan your itinerary, book your tickets, and get ready to experience the best of what this charming country has to offer.

MUST DO'S IN THE NETHERLANDS

There is no shortage of things to do and see in this wonderful country. Here are some of the must-do's when visiting the Netherlands:

1. Visit Amsterdam: Amsterdam is the capital of the Netherlands and a must-visit destination. This vibrant city is home to world-famous museums, including the Rijksmuseum and the Van Gogh Museum, as well as the stunning canals that run

throughout the city. Take a boat tour through the canals for a unique perspective of the city and its architecture.

2. See the tulips in Keukenhof Gardens: Keukenhof Gardens is one of the largest flower gardens in the world, and is especially famous for its tulips. This park is open from mid-April to mid-May and is a must-visit during the tulip season. Visitors can admire over seven million tulips in a variety of colours and shapes, making it a truly breathtaking experience.

3. Explore the Windmills of Kinderdijk: Kinderdijk is a village located in the

province of South Holland, and is famous for its 19 windmills that were built in the 18th century. These windmills were used to pump water from the low-lying polders to prevent the surrounding land from flooding. Today, visitors can tour the windmills and learn about the important role they played in the history of the Netherlands.

4. Visit the Zaanse Schans: The Zaanse Schans is an open-air museum located near Amsterdam. This historic village is home to a number of historic windmills, houses, and workshops that have been carefully restored and

preserved. Visitors can take a tour of the windmills and learn about traditional Dutch crafts, such as cheese making and woodworking.

5. Take a bike tour: The Netherlands is known for its bike-friendly cities, and cycling is a popular mode of transportation. Take a bike tour of one of the cities, such as Amsterdam or Utrecht, to see the sights and experience the local culture.

6. Visit the Royal Palace of Amsterdam: The Royal Palace of Amsterdam is a stunning building located in the heart of the city. This palace was originally built as a town hall in the 17th century

and was later converted into a palace. Today, visitors can tour the palace and admire its impressive architecture and art collection.

7. Explore the Markthal: The Markthal is a covered market located in Rotterdam. This modern building is home to a variety of food stalls, shops, and restaurants, making it a great place to sample local cuisine and shop for unique gifts.

8. Visit the Deltapark Neeltje Jans: The Deltapark Neeltje Jans is a theme park located on the island of Schouwen-Duiveland. This park is dedicated to the history and

technology of the Dutch delta works and offers visitors the chance to experience the Delta works in a fun and interactive way.

9. Explore the Hague: The Hague is the third largest city in the Netherlands and is home to several important international organisations, including the International Criminal Court and the International Court of Justice. Visitors can tour these organisations, as well as the many museums and art galleries in the city, including the Peace Palace and the Mauritshuis Museum.

10. Enjoy a cheese tasting: The Netherlands is famous for its cheese, and a cheese tasting is a must-do for any food lover. Try a variety of Dutch cheeses, including Gouda, Edam, Leiden, and learn about the history and production of this delicious dairy product.

11. Visit the Dutch beaches: The Netherlands is home to several beautiful beaches, including the North Sea beaches of Zandvoort, Noordwijk, and Scheveningen. These beaches are popular destinations for sunbathing, swimming, and water sports.

12. Walk through the Red Light District: The Red Light District in Amsterdam is a notorious neighbourhood known for its sex workers and sex-oriented businesses. Although this area may not be suitable for everyone, it is an important part of Amsterdam's history and culture. Visitors can take a guided tour of the district to learn about its history and its current state.

13. Explore the Dutch countryside: The Netherlands is home to some beautiful countryside, including the Veluwe region and the rural areas of Friesland and Drenthe. Take a drive through the countryside to see the rolling hills,

farmland, and traditional Dutch villages.

14. Visit a Dutch cheese market: The Dutch cheese markets are a unique aspect of Dutch culture and a must-visit for any traveller. These markets are held weekly in various cities, including Alkmaar, Gouda, and Edam, and offer visitors the chance to sample and purchase traditional Dutch cheeses.

15. Take a scenic canal cruise: The canals of the Netherlands are a major part of the country's history and culture, and a canal cruise is a great way to see the cities and countryside. Visitors can

take a scenic boat tour through the canals to admire the stunning architecture and landscapes.

These are just some of the many must-do activities in the Netherlands. Whether you're interested in history, culture, food, or nature, this wonderful country has something for everyone. With its beautiful landscapes, rich history, and vibrant culture, the Netherlands is a must-visit destination for any traveller.

HELPFUL NETHERLAND PHRASES

As a tourist or a visitor, learning a few basic Dutch phrases can be extremely helpful and make your visit even more enjoyable. Here are some of the most useful Dutch phrases you can use while you are in the Netherlands:

1. Hallo - Hello
2. Dag - Hi/Bye
3. Hoe gaat het? - How are you?
4. Goed, dank je. En met jou? - Good, thank you. And with you?
5. Sorry - Sorry
6. Alstublieft - Please
7. Dank je wel - Thank you very much
8. Graag gedaan - You're welcome
9. Ja - Yes
10. Nee - No

11. Ik spreek geen Nederlands - I don't speak Dutch

12. Spreekt u Engels? - Do you speak English?

13. Ik begrijp het niet - I don't understand

14. Wilt u iets drinken? - Would you like something to drink?

15. Waar is het toilet? - Where is the toilet?

16. Hoeveel kost dat? - How much does it cost?

17. Ik wil graag - I would like to

18. Ik heb honger - I'm hungry

19. Ik heb dorst - I'm thirsty

20. Hoe laat is het? - What time is it?

When ordering food or drinks, you may come across some common Dutch terms:

1. Een biertje - A beer
2. Een wijntje - A glass of wine
3. Een koffie - A coffee
4. Een water - A water
5. Een bittergarnituur - A snack mix
6. Een kaasplankje - A cheese platter

When shopping, these phrases might come in handy:

1. Ik wil graag - I would like to
2. Hoeveel kost dat? - How much does it cost?

3. Hoeveel kosten deze schoenen? - How much do these shoes cost?

4. Hoeveel kosten deze broek? - How much does this pants cost?

5. Heeft u deze in een andere maat? - Do you have this in another size?

6. Heeft u deze in een andere kleur? - Do you have this in another color?

7. Ik wil graag iets terugbrengen - I would like to return something

When travelling on public transportation, you might find these phrases helpful:

1. Waar is de dichtstbijzijnde bushalte? - Where is the nearest bus stop?

2. Hoe kom ik naar het centrum? - How do I get to the city center?

3. Hoeveel kost een kaartje? - How much does a ticket cost?

4. Hoe laat vertrekt de volgende trein? - What time does the next train leave?

5. Hoe laat komt de volgende trein aan? - What time does the next train arrive?

Finally, it's always helpful to know a few basic numbers:

1. Een - 1
2. Twee - 2
3. Drie - 3
4. Vier - 4

5. Vijf - 5

6. Zes - 6

7. Zeven - 7

8. Acht - 8

9. Negen - 9

10.   Tien - 10

Remember, even if you only know a few Dutch phrases, the locals will appreciate the effort you are making to speak their language and will be more willing to help you with anything you need. Don't be afraid to make mistakes, they are part of the learning process.

knowing a few Dutch phrases can greatly enhance your experience while visiting the

Netherlands. Whether you're ordering food, shopping, using public transportation, or just trying to navigate your way around the country, having a basic knowledge of the language will make your visit smoother and more enjoyable.

CHAPTER THREE

ACCOMMODATION

BEST PLACES TO EAT, SLEEP AND RELAX

Here are some of the best places for each of these activities in the Netherlands:

EATING:

1. De Bakkerswinkel: This bakery-café chain serves delicious pastries, cakes, sandwiches, and coffee in a cosy and welcoming atmosphere.
2. Foodhallen Amsterdam: A former tram depot turned into a trendy food market, Foodhallen offers a variety of international cuisine and local specialties, making it a great place to try something new.
3. De Pelgrim: This restaurant in Rotterdam serves Dutch cuisine with a

modern twist, using locally sourced ingredients and traditional recipes.

4. De Waaghals: A popular vegetarian restaurant in Amsterdam, De Waaghals offers creative and flavorful plant-based dishes.

5. Rijsttafel Restaurant LeASI: This Indonesian restaurant in Rotterdam serves a traditional Indonesian rice table, a feast of small dishes served with rice.

SLEEPING:

1. The Dylan Amsterdam: This 5-star luxury hotel in Amsterdam's canal district offers elegant rooms, a spa, and a Michelin-starred restaurant.

2. CitizenM Hotel Rotterdam: A stylish and affordable hotel in the heart of Rotterdam, CitizenM offers comfortable rooms with modern amenities.

3. Hotel De Mallemoolen: A charming hotel in Amsterdam's Jordaan neighbourhood, Hotel De Mallemoolen is housed in a 17th-century building and features antique furnishings.
4. Hotel De Goudfazant: A hotel in Amsterdam's trendy NDSM wharf neighbourhood, Hotel De Goudfazant offers unique rooms in a converted shipping container and a spacious outdoor terrace.
5. Hotel Kasteel De Berckt: A castle hotel in the southern Netherlands, Hotel Kasteel De Berckt offers luxurious rooms and suites, a swimming pool, and a restaurant serving French cuisine.

RELAXING:

1. Keukenhof Gardens: Located in Lisse, the Keukenhof Gardens are one of the largest flower gardens in the world, featuring over 7 million tulips, daffodils, and other flowers.

2. De Hoge Veluwe National Park: This national park in the central Netherlands offers a mix of forests, heathlands, and sand dunes, making it a great place for hiking and wildlife spotting.

3. Thermae 2000: This thermal bath complex in Valkenburg offers a variety of indoor and outdoor pools, steam rooms, and saunas, as well as massage treatments and beauty services.

4. Spa Zuiver: A spa in Amsterdam, Spa Zuiver offers a range of wellness facilities, including hot tubs, saunas, and massage rooms, as well as a restaurant serving healthy cuisine.

5. Zandvoort Beach: Located on the North Sea coast, Zandvoort is a popular beach resort known for its

sandy beaches, dunes, and vibrant atmosphere.

These are just a few of the many options for eating, sleeping, and relaxing in the Netherlands. Whether you're looking for a gourmet meal, a luxurious stay, or a chance to unwind and recharge, you're sure to find what you're looking for in this beautiful country.

ENTERTAINMENT AND NIGHTLIFE

With its bustling cities, lively nightlife, and diverse cultural offerings, the Netherlands is a popular destination for visitors looking for a fun and lively entertainment scene.

One of the main hubs of nightlife and entertainment in the Netherlands is Amsterdam, the country's capital and largest city. Amsterdam is renowned for its vibrant nightlife, with a wide range of bars, clubs, and music venues catering to a diverse range of musical tastes. Whether you're into electronic dance music, hip-hop, live jazz, or anything in between, you're sure to find a venue that caters to your tastes in Amsterdam.

One of the most famous nightlife spots in Amsterdam is the Leidseplein, a bustling square in the heart of the city that is surrounded by bars, clubs, and cafes. Leidseplein is a popular spot for locals and tourists alike, and it's a great place to grab a drink, listen to live music, or dance the night away. Another popular spot for nightlife in Amsterdam is the Rembrandtplein, which is known for its lively atmosphere and its many bars and clubs.

If you're interested in live music, Amsterdam has a thriving music scene, with many venues offering concerts and performances by local and international artists. Some of the most popular music venues in the city include the Paradiso, Melkweg, and the Bimhuis. These venues host a wide range of musical genres, from rock and pop to jazz and classical.

In addition to its nightlife and music scene, the Netherlands is also known for its rich cultural heritage and its many museums and art galleries. Amsterdam is home to a number of world-class museums, including the Van Gogh Museum, the Rijksmuseum, and the Stedelijk Museum, all of which showcase the works of some of the world's most famous artists.

Aside from Amsterdam, there are many other cities in the Netherlands that offer a rich entertainment and nightlife scene. Rotterdam, the second-largest city in the country, is known for its cutting-edge architecture and its vibrant nightlife. Rotterdam has a thriving music scene, with many venues offering live music and DJ performances. The city is also home to a number of cultural institutions, including the Museum Boijmans Van Beuningen and the Kunsthal, which showcase the works of local and international artists.

In the southern Netherlands, the city of Eindhoven is known for its lively entertainment scene, with many bars, clubs, and music venues catering to a wide range of musical tastes. Eindhoven is also home to the famous Dutch Design Week, an annual festival that showcases the latest and greatest in Dutch design, technology, and innovation.

Another city in the Netherlands that is known for its rich cultural heritage is Utrecht, which is home to many museums and art galleries, as well as a thriving music scene. The city is also home to the TivoliVredenburg, a large concert venue that hosts performances by local and international artists.

In addition to its cities, the Netherlands is also home to a number of festivals and events that are worth checking out if you're interested in entertainment and nightlife. The Lowlands Festival, for example, is one of the largest music festivals in the country, attracting thousands of visitors every year. The festival features performances by some of the biggest names in music, as well as a variety of other entertainment, including theatre, comedy, and dance.

The Netherlands is also home to a number of other festivals and events that celebrate its cultural heritage, such as the tulip festival in Keukenhof, the flower fields in the region of Bollenstreek, and the famous cheese market in Alkmaar. These events are a great way to experience the unique traditions and customs of the Netherlands, and to learn about the country's rich cultural heritage.

Another popular event in the Netherlands is the King's Day, a national holiday that celebrates the birthday of the King. The holiday is marked by a series of festivals and events throughout the country, including street parties, music performances, and boat parades. King's Day is a great opportunity to experience Dutch culture and its love for festivities, as the entire country comes alive with music, food, drinks, and entertainment.

The Netherlands is a great destination for those looking for a fun and lively entertainment scene. With its rich cultural heritage, vibrant nightlife, and diverse range of festivals and events, the country offers something for everyone, from music lovers to art enthusiasts. Whether you're looking to dance the night away, explore world-class museums, or simply enjoy the sights and sounds of a bustling city, the Netherlands is a destination that should not be missed.

CHAPTER FOUR

FUN FACTS ABOUT NETHERLANDS

The Netherlands is a small country located in Western Europe with a rich cultural heritage and history. Here are some interesting facts about this unique country:

1. Tulips: The Netherlands is famous for its tulips and is the largest exporter of tulip bulbs in the world. Tulips were first introduced to the Netherlands in the 16th century and have since become a symbol of the country.

2. Windmills: The Netherlands is home to over 1,000 windmills, many of which are still in use today. These iconic structures were originally used to pump water from the low-lying areas of the country, but now some are used to generate electricity.

3. Water Management: The Netherlands is famous for its water management system, which helps to keep the country dry even though much of it is below sea level. A network of dikes, dams, and canals helps to prevent

floods and protect the country from the North Sea.

4. Bicycles: The Netherlands is one of the most bicycle-friendly countries in the world. Nearly half of all trips in the country are made by bicycle and the country has an extensive network of bike lanes and paths.

5. Cheese: The Netherlands is famous for its cheese, particularly Gouda and Edam. These cheeses are made from cow's milk and are known for their mild, nutty flavour.

6. The Dutch Golden Age: The Dutch Golden Age was a period of great prosperity in the 17th century during which the Netherlands became one of the wealthiest and most influential countries in the world. During this time, the country experienced a cultural and artistic boom, and many great masterpieces of art and architecture were produced.

7. The Dutch East India Company: The Dutch East India Company was a powerful trading company established in the 17th century. It was one of the first multinational corporations and played a major role in the globalisation of trade and commerce.

8. The Dutch West India Company: The Dutch West India Company was another powerful trading company established in the 17th century. It was involved in the colonization of the Americas and played a major role in the transatlantic slave trade.

9. Vincent van Gogh: Vincent van Gogh is one of the most famous artists of all time and was born in the Netherlands. He is known for his distinctive style and his use of bold, vibrant colours. He is considered one of the pioneers of modern art.

10. Anne Frank: Anne Frank is one of the most well-known victims of the Holocaust. She was a Jewish girl who

lived in Amsterdam during World War II and wrote a diary about her experiences in hiding. Her diary has become a symbol of the horrors of the Holocaust and a testament to the human spirit.

11. Delft Blue: Delft Blue is a type of blue and white pottery that is associated with the Netherlands. It is known for its intricate designs and is a popular souvenir for tourists.

12. Heineken: Heineken is a well-known brand of beer that originated in the Netherlands. The brewery was established in 1864 and today, Heineken is one of the largest beer producers in the world.

13. Royal Family: The Netherlands has a monarchy and the current king is King Willem-Alexander. The Dutch monarchy is one of the oldest in the world and has a rich history.

14. The Dutch Language: The Dutch language is a Germanic language that

is spoken by over 20 million people worldwide. It is the official language of the Netherlands and is also spoken in Belgium, Suriname, and the Netherlands Antilles.

15. The Dutch Economy: The Netherlands is one of the richest countries in the world and has a strong and diverse economy. The country is known for its strong agricultural sector, as well as for its shipping and logistics industries. The Netherlands is also a hub for international trade and is home to many multinational corporations.

16. The Hague: The Hague is the seat of the Dutch government and is home to many international courts and organisations, including the International Criminal Court and the International Court of Justice. The city is often referred to as the "legal capital of the world."

17. Amsterdam: Amsterdam is the capital and largest city of the Netherlands. It is known for its canals, museums, and rich cultural heritage. Amsterdam is also famous for its vibrant nightlife and coffee shops, where marijuana is legally sold.

18. Wooden Shoes: Wooden shoes, also known as clogs, are a traditional type of footwear that are associated with the Netherlands. They were originally worn by farmers and workers, but today they are mostly used as a symbol of Dutch culture.

19. KLM: KLM is the flag carrier airline of the Netherlands and is one of the oldest airlines in the world. KLM was established in 1919 and today, it is a member of the SkyTeam global airline alliance.

20. The Dutch Education System: The Dutch education system is known for its high quality and is considered one of the best in the world. The country

has a strong tradition of public education and is home to many world-renowned universities, including the University of Amsterdam and the Technical University of Delft.

21. The Dutch Football Team: The Dutch football team, also known as the Oranje, is one of the most successful national teams in Europe. The team has a rich history of success and is known for its attacking style of play.

These are just a few of the many interesting facts about the Netherlands. From its rich cultural heritage to its modern-day innovations, the country continues to be a fascinating place with a unique identity and a proud history. Whether you're a history buff, an art lover, or simply someone who enjoys learning about new places, the Netherlands is a destination that is sure to leave a lasting impression.